always shine your
pearl beautiful mama!

Shuck with ♡
Jessica

To my parents, who have sacrificed so much so I could live my best life.

To Steve, who is my favorite letter "S".

To Pearl, who inspires me to shine.

To Archer, who motivates me to aim for the stars.

To Drs. Ron and Mary Hulnick, who gave me the freedom to be me.

To Dr. Robert Holden, who showed me how to lead with love.

To Stacey, who brings my ideas to life in the most shucktacular ways.

To everyone who has been part of my shucking story, thank you.

Front cover, book design and illustrations by Stacey Uy.

Pictures by Studio Luniste.

Printed by Ingram Content Group in the United States of America.

First printing, 2021.

Life Shucker
1155 Camino Del Mar #469
Del Mar, CA 92014

www.lifeshucker.com

SHUCK THIS WAY

44 WAYS TO SHUCK OPEN YOUR SHELL AND SHINE!

BY JESSICA ZEMPLE

DESIGNED AND ILLUSTRATED BY STACEY UY

SHUCK
WITH
LOVE

YOU ARE A PEARL.

It is the essence, the heart, of who you are. The radiance of your pearl was created by layers of strength through the grit of life's experiences. Your pearl is unique and has so much shucking beauty to offer the world.

EVERY PEARL HAS A SHELL.

When life brings challenges we often close the shell around our pearl to protect our self. This is natural, and sometimes appropriate, for healing.

EVERY SHELL NEEDS TO BE SHUCKED.

The problem is if your shell is closed too long it creates a barrier between you and the world making you feel disconnected to yourself and others. Eventually, the once protective shell starts to hold you back from reaching your greatest potential. The only way to shuck open someone's shell, or your own, is through love.

YOU ARE A SHUCKER.

Whether you are four or 104 years old you can Shuck This Way! Use these forty-four simple, yet powerful life skills, based on love, to shuck open your shell to let your pearl shine!

The Shuck This Way life skills are centered on your mind, body, and soul to let your life flow. Use them for yourself. Use them for others. Just remember, the shell is the limitation of your world until you shuck it. You will then be open to a sea of possibilities.

Now, go shuck yourself and everyone you know!

SILENCE

In the busyness of our world it is rare that we actually get time to think and reflect on what is important. Silence is a beautiful gift we can give someone to allow them to explore what is truly present for them to support them on their journey of greater fulfillment and equanimity.

Please know that silence can be awkward for people. When listening to someone be mindful not to interject any pearls of wisdom to change the awkwardness. The silence is an invitation for the person you are with to go deeper in to their heart and find the why behind the why. It is in the silence where the truth comes forward.

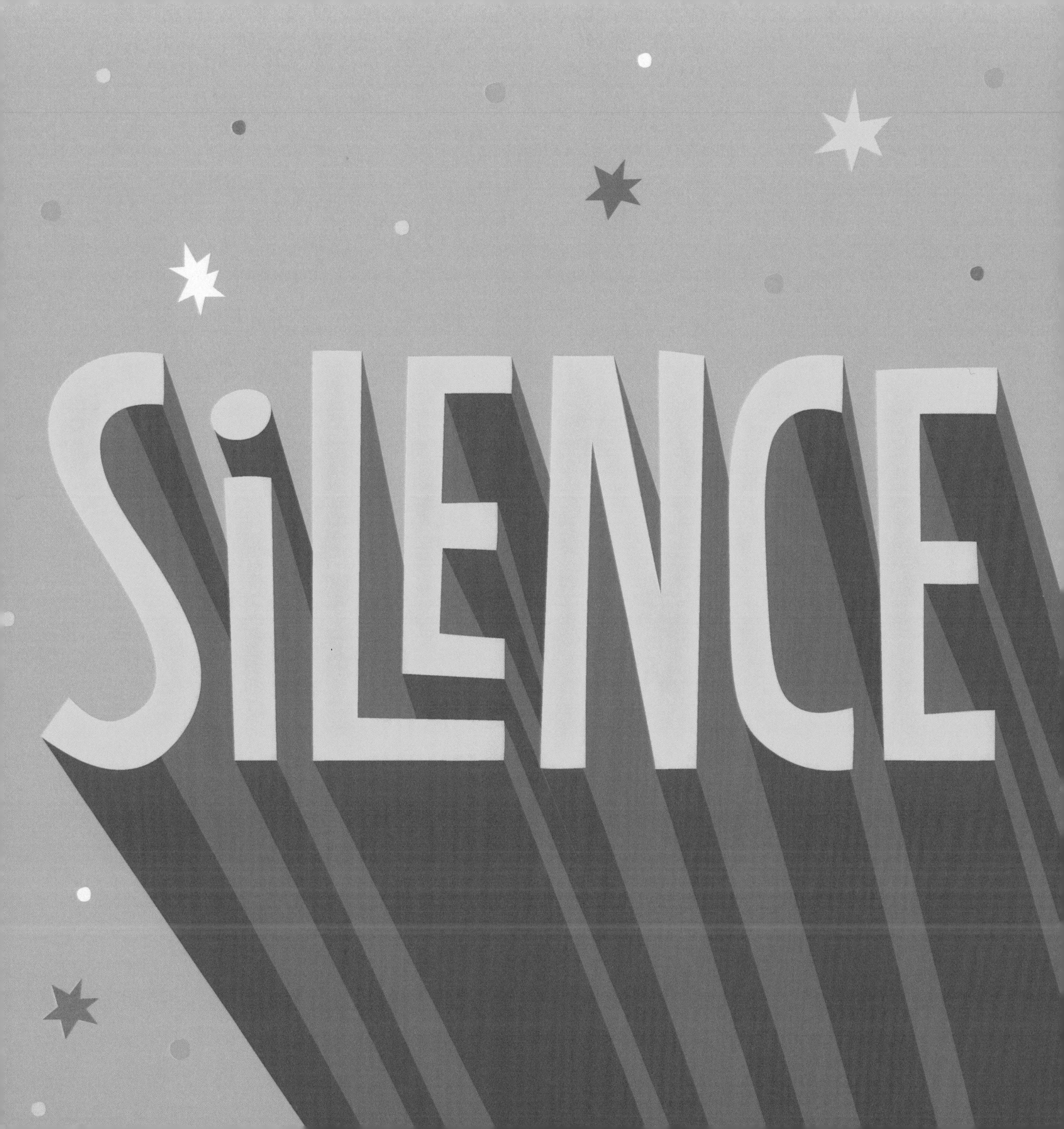
SiLENCE

LISTEN WITH LOVE

So often people are not truly listening. Their mind may be on what they have to do next or thinking about what they are going to say. Be present. When you truly give someone time to speak from their heart you will be amazed at the insights that will come forward benefiting both of you.

LISTEN WITH LOVE

BE PRESENT

Listening to your heart is the key to a meaningful life. When you are connecting with your heart, or helping someone else connect with theirs, it is instrumental to be present. Find a place and time where you can sit in stillness even if it is just for a single minute. Give yourself permission to be in this very moment by putting any worries aside.

Ask yourself what is it I need to know right now? Then listen.

Sit in stillness to let what you already know flow.

THE GRACE OF SPACE

In our fast-paced world, we often wonder why things are not moving as fast as we think we want them to whether it be a promotion or your next date. Often we think the perceived delay is something negative.

What if the extra time was for you? What could you do with this time?

There is an element of faith that needs to occur in the grace of space. Can you trust that this time is divine? Remember there is a lot more happening in the world than we can see. Trust in the process and the time in between will start to be a gift as opposed to an anecdote of anxiety.

THE
GRACE
OF
SPACE

REFLECT WHAT YOU HEAR

When listening to someone repeat back what you hear to ensure you truly understand what the other person is saying. This allows you to get to the heart of what truly matters by avoiding any miscommunication.

This could be, "What I hear you saying is XYZ. Is that correct?" or "Let me see if I am hearing you correctly. Are you saying XYZ?"

REFLECT

what you

HEAR

CONFIRM WHAT YOU HEARD

Even if you think you are a master communicator it does not mean what you say has been heard in the way you intended. People hear through their own filters that have been uniquely developed through their life's experiences. While we may be using the same words they often have different meanings to different people. Ask the person you are talking to repeat what they heard by saying something like, "Could you tell me how that came across to you?" or "What did you hear in what I was saying?" Not only will this ensure you are in alignment, this will also give you insight in to what the other person is thinking.

CONFIRM WHAT YOU HEARD

SLOW DOWN TO SPEED UP

In a world where we are moving at the speed of busyness slowing someone down can be the greatest gift. By slowing someone down it gives them space and time to tune in to their hearts and intuition. As they do they can make choices more aligned with their life leading to greater results by being in their flow.

Plus, when people are in a constant state of chaos it is easy to make mistakes or miss opportunities. By slowing life down you will recognize more opportunities and, ironically, find that you get to your dream faster.

SLOW

down

— TO

SPEED

up

APPLY A PAUSE TO LISTEN

Are you a YES person? Are you eager to please everyone and in the process your dreams get lost? If you are, there might be an automatic response to every request you get which is YES! Of course I'll do it (even though you are cringing inside).

The automatic YES needs to stop now. You are much too important to be prioritizing everyone else above yourself.

The next time you get a request I invite you to pause to really listen to your heart. All you have to do is say, "I need to think about this and will get back to you." That's it! Then, see what your heart says!

APPLY
A
PAUSE
TO
Listen

ASK PERMISSION

Before you coach or offer advice to someone it is critical to ask permission. This shows them respect and gives them an invitation to say no. It is rare in our society to feel like we can say no. Saying no is helpful because sometimes people are not in a place to really listen. Asking permission also softens people's defense mechanisms allowing them to be more vulnerable and truly hear what loving words you have to share.

ASK
PERMISSION

IDENTIFY THE REAL REQUEST

Some people LOVE to complain. The key is underneath every complaint there is a request. There is something the person wants or needs yet has not articulated what it is. You can really support someone by helping them identify what their real request is. When someone walks away from the conversation with an actual request or insight they will feel empowered to act.

IDENTIFY

THE REAL request

FIND THE REAL DREAM

There is generally more than meets the eye when helping someone go for their dreams. Often people will say they want one thing and are confused or frustrated it has not happened. Keep asking, "What is it you really, really, really want?"

Sometimes they may need to take more inspired action. Other times people's real dreams may be covered by layers of fear and they are not truly going for what they want in life.

When you can help them through the fear they might actually be surprised, or even relieved, at what comes from their heart. They will feel more motivation since they are starting where it matters most—their real dream.

FIND THE REAL DREAM

ASK WHY THEY ARE ASKING

The answer to most people's questions is actually in the question itself.

The next time someone asks you a question instead of answering ask them "what makes you ask that?" You may find they are wondering about something totally different than how you were going to answer the question.

Often people are afraid to share what is really in their hearts for a number of reasons. By inviting them to open up it takes the conversation to a whole new level.

ask **WHY**

THEY ARE ASKING

LET PEOPLE COMPLETE THEIR THOUGHTS

So often we think we know what someone will say and it is hardly ever right. Why? Because no one sees the world the same way you do. Thank goodness they don't! You already know how you think. Why not listen to what other people have to say!

Let other people complete their thoughts. It takes courage for many people to share openly and authentically. You speeding up the conversation by completing their sentence only suppresses the opportunities and may even cause someone to close their shell. By slowing down and letting people explore their own thoughts, you can help them get to the core of what they are looking for. Plus, you might even learn something along the way!

Let

PEOPLE
COMPLETE
THEIR

THOUGHTS

GUIDE PEOPLE TO DISCOVER THEIR OWN PEARLS

Each person has their own wisdom to resolve many of the questions they are seeking to answer. Yet we want to give advice to people all the time. We want to prevent people from making our mistakes. We want to feel helpful. We want to save time.

While there are times advice is appropriate check in to see if that time is now. This is not about you. It is about them. Is this a time you can guide them in finding their own pearls of wisdom? Remember a truth discovered is always better than a truth told.

GUIDE
PEOPLE TO
DISCOVER
THEIR OWN
PEARLS

MEET THEM AT THEIR FEAR

So often we invalidate people's fears. It comes in the form of "Oh, don't worry about that" or "It could be worse." This makes people feel misunderstood, alone, or even wrong for feeling how they do.

The reality is the fear is real to them no matter how you see the scenario. Instead, let them know their fears are valid. Let them know their feelings are valid. By doing this you acknowledge them for what is true for them. You can then start talking about possibilities of moving through the fear because you are starting from the same place and what really matters to the person in front of you.

MEET THEM

AT THEIR FEAR

STAY OUT OF THE STORY

People LOVE helping people. Somewhere in society we learned that if we sympathize with people that we are helping them. In truth you are adding more fuel to the fire making them a victim.

If you can stay out of the story while listening to someone, this will empower them to move through any of life's challenges with more grace and ease.

STAY OUT
OF THE
STORY

LISTEN FOR LABELS

Any time someone labels themselves or others it is disabling. Labels tend to confine a person in to a certain set of expectations and assumptions that have been developed by one's learning through experience, role models, or society. By highlighting labels the person is using this will assist in opening up possibility of experiencing other people and your own life in a new way.

Listen

FOR

LABELS

PERMISSION TO DREAM BIG

Most people never give themselves permission to dream big and go for what they really want in life. You can create a safe place for them to explore what is truly in their heart. Remind them that they are worthy of what their dream is. You can then help them in taking action to make it happen!

Once you actually know what you are going for it is a lot easier to take inspired action in the direction of your dreams and living your greatest life.

PERMISSION TO
DREAM
BIG

STRETCH YOURSELF

Many people are afraid of failure so they set their goals way too low. The problem with that is if you achieve your goal you will miss how far you truly can go. Set a goal that is a little scary and uncomfortable, yet still believable. Stretch your mind for what is possible and take action to make it true.

STRETCH
YOURSELF

BE KIND TO YOURSELF

We are often our toughest critics. We can nitpick the smallest or even unimportant details just to be hard on ourselves. This only leads to lower self esteem making life more challenging than it needs to be.

One way to boost yourself esteem is stop with all the negative self talk. Start treating yourself like you would a precious little child that is learning and growing. Why? YOU are learning and growing every single day. Be gentle and kind to yourself and you will experience greater confidence and joy in your heart allowing you to shine even more.

BE kind

TO YOUR SELF

YOU SEE WHAT YOU ARE LOOKING FOR

Our minds are powerful. We can find evidence for anything we want to support in our mind. If you think someone is out to get you then that is what you will see. Our creative mind will make the littlest things add up to something big.

If you want to change how life is for you it is important to start looking for new evidence. What if you looked for ways that person is helping you (even if not intentional on their part)? How would that change your feelings? How would that change your life? Try it today and I imagine you might be surprised at what you see.

YOU SEE WHAT YOU ARE LOOKING FOR

SHINE A LIGHT ON LIMITING BELIEFS

Limiting beliefs are obstacles for living our fullest potential. When you hear someone's limiting belief it is an opportunity for you to show them where there is a new way of thinking that could lead to a desired change in their life.

Some ways to identify limiting beliefs are listening for absolutes (I could *never* ask for help), shoulds (I *should* go to the event), or labels (I am an introvert). All of these will lead someone down a path that is not theirs to follow. Help them see new possibilities so they can live the life that is true to their heart.

SHINE A LIGHT ON

LIMITING
BELIEFS

TRUST THE CHAOS OF THE CONVERSATION

When coaching you will find that the conversation can jump all over the place. Sometimes it is someone avoiding the real opportunity. It could also be that the disparate stories are actually interconnected and when woven together the bigger vision can be seen.

Listen deeply. Tap in to your intuition to guide them back to the heart of the matter. Or, help them see the beautiful tapestry being woven together by the previously unconnected stories.

TRUST
THE CHAOS
OF THE CONVERSATION

REFRAME AN ISSUE AS AN OPPORTUNITY

Mindset matters. If you see a challenging situation as a problem, burden, or road block that is what it will be. On the other hand, if you look at life as though it is happening for you then you will see the beauty of all aspects of life.

We are only given what we can handle so you are more than prepared to tackle anything. This does not mean it will be easy. It does mean you can do it with a supportive mindset.

REFRAME AN ISSUE AS AN *opportunity*

CHOOSE YOUR THOUGHTS

Everyone has an endless stream of thoughts. Everyone also has the choice of what thoughts to focus on. You can focus on the thoughts that keeps your shell closed and see what that does for your health and well being. OR, you can choose the thoughts that inspire and motivate you to keep your shell open and see what that does for your health and well being.

Look at each thought passing through and evaluate what that particular thought is doing for you. Is it one you want to hold on to? Or, is it one you would like to let go of? It's your choice.

CHOOSE YOUR THOUGHTS

FIND INFINITE POSSIBILITIES

When you feel like there is only one way to solve a problem or move forward you are missing infinite possibilities. Often we only see possibilities based on our experiences, belief systems, and knowledge limiting us in choices for creating our best life. In order to change this you must look for new possibilities. By seeking them out this will actually help you find them. There is way more to this life than we know. When you look for it that is when you will find it.

FIND
INFINITE
POSSIBILITIES

SIX NEW POSSIBILITIES

Getting stuck happens. When you are stuck in an unfavorable story it is time to write a new script. Any time you find yourself stuck on repeat, challenge yourself to create six new possibilities. Let your imagination go. Write a script that is in your favor though. Life is happening for you. Why would you tell yourself otherwise? When you see new possibilities, the unfavorable story stops.

Change the script. Change your life.

NEW POSSIBILITIES

6

REDEFINE FAILURE

Many people in the world are afraid to fail. They tie their worthiness, or lack thereof, to failure holding them back from taking any worthwhile risks. Why would failure have anything to do with your worthiness? You are worthy because you were born. Everyone matters. Especially you.

What is failure anyway? Failure is that you tried something and did not work out the way you expected it to. What if it worked out exactly how it was supposed to? What if failure is the world's way to guide you in a new direction that is more aligned with your path? I encourage you to look at failure in a new way and see how that impacts your willingness to take more risks.

All of that being said, please be honest with yourself. Did you truly put in your best effort for success? If not, take inspired action to change that now. And, if you did, kudos for you for trying!

REDEFINE
fAILURE

LIVE IN GRATITUDE

The attitude of gratitude is so cliché and so life changing. Find gratitude in even the grittiest of situations and I guarantee it will have a positive impact on your life.

Live IN GRATITUDE

BODY

SET AN INTENTION

An intention is a declaration of what it is you want to feel or experience. Clear, positive intention involves clarity of purpose and the willingness to act on it.

When you hold a clear intention, your thoughts, feelings, and behaviors—including your words—align. All your choices are now in the direction of what you want to experience.

Where your attention goes, grows. By being clear with what you want to focus on that will assist you in bringing that to life.

SET AN

INTENTION

ASK FOR WHAT YOU WANT

Many people were raised thinking that asking for what you want is rude, egotistical, or selfish. This leads to people not truly asking for what they want. Or worse, expecting others to know what they want and then get disappointed when they can't read their minds.

It is time to change your perspective that asking for what you want is a birthright. Sure, someone can say no. Without asking though you will never know.

ASK FOR *what* YOU WANT

ACT ON INSPIRATION

Our hearts know what we want and our head can often make up the silliest stories to stop us. Instead of giving your mind time to make up all the reasons you should *not* do something, act on the inspiration you have. When you do, you'll see all the brilliance in store for you!

ACT ON

INSPIR-ATION!

COMPLETE ACHIEVABLE STEPS

Once you get clear on what the vision is for the future it is now time to get there. Often people will paralyze themselves trying to figure out how to get to their goal since it seems so far and perhaps even unreachable if the dream is BIG and BOLD.

The key is identifying achievable steps. By committing to, and completing, achievable steps it will build your momentum and courage supporting you on your way to your dream. Just think, if you take one small action toward your dream every day in one year you will have done 365 things!

COMPLETE ACHIEVABLE STEPS

TAKE INSPIRED ACTION

People often confuse busy with productive. They do things just to do things. When you are creating your best life it is critical to choose actions that are aligned with your goals. Determine what you need to do to move closer to your dreams and do it. Stop wasting your time on things that do not matter. You only have so much energy in this world and why not use it towards living your best life?

TAKE *Inspired* ACTION

PRIORITY CHECK

I love when clients come to me and say, "I am just not getting anywhere with <INSERT DREAM HERE>." I then ask what a typical day looks like for them. I hear them run through this and that. I then listen as they prioritize everyone and everything else above their dream. Hmm, I can't imagine why you are not realizing your dream?

It's time. You need to spend time on your dream. When you do it is as if you are putting a stake in the ground and telling the universe, "I am ready!" Try it and see what happens.

priority ✔CHECK

LOOK AT WHERE YOUR COMMITMENTS ARE

Some people think they are going towards their dream and get frustrated or disappointed when they cannot seem to get there. The reason may be that they are not truly committed to what they say they are.

Look at where their commitments are to see what the goals are at this point in time. The goal they are going for may be unconscious. Slowing someone down to really see what they are committed to by looking at what is happening in their life will help them see why their life is the way it is. They can then let go of their frustration and disappointment or they can make new commitments.

LOOK AT WHERE YOUR

COMMITMENTS

ARE

MAKE A COMMITMENT

Commitment leads to success. Commitment is what powers you through your fears. Commitment keeps you motivated when times are tough. Commitment drives your choices and actions. Commitment brings unexpected opportunities to you. Commitment shows the world you are serious about living your best life. Commitment is what makes your dream a reality. Commit to committing today!

EXPERIMENT

It can be scary to commit to something you are not sure about. Instead, see if you like something before you make a big commitment. Experiment!

Just like someone would do with dating. You date to see if you and the other person are the perfect fit. If the date is good you go on another one. If it is not, you don't. Well, at least I hope you don't. Eventually you can make the commitment to get married. You do NOT need to know if you will be marrying the person on the first date.

The same is true with so many choices in life. We put unnecessary pressure on our decisions that it paralyzes us. We think we have to jump both feet in. At times that is appropriate. But, not all. Experiment to see if you want to make a commitment to something new.

EXPER -IMENT

UNCOVER COMPETING INTENTIONS

Are you having a hard time reaching your goal? You could be running in to competing intentions. This is when different intentions or belief systems conflict making it next to impossible to reach your goal. For example, if you were raised to always clean your plate it may be hard to lose weight by reducing calories.

Help to identify competing intentions by asking, "what is it holding me back from my goal?"

Once you identify the competing intentions you can untangle them by making changes to your goals, belief systems, or behaviors to support you in creating your own success!

uncover
— COMPETING —
INTENTIONS

BEFRIEND REJECTION

Rejection makes people uneasy. They think the rejection is somehow personal and tied to their self worth. What if rejection was just rejection? What if it had nothing to do with your value? When you are courageous enough to ask for what you want in this life you will get a no. Keep going. Make rejection your friend as opposed to an obstacle in living the life that lights you up.

BEFRIEND

★ REJECTION ★

RECONNECT WITH CREATIVITY

When did life get so serious? Let that inner child out and let the creativity flow! Creativity is in everyone. All we have to do is let it come forward. Challenge yourself to do one creative thing today whether it is driving a new way home or making a new dinner recipe. Creativity breeds more creativity. Start tapping in to it and see where it goes!

RECONNECT

with

CREATIVITY

ACKNOWLEDGE PEOPLE

At the end of the day we all just want to be seen. Show the people around you that you truly see them by taking time to acknowledge them for what you have seen or experienced with them.

It can be as simple as saying, "I so appreciate you for taking out the garbage," or "You always turn your reports in on time and I really appreciate that because it makes my life easier. Thank you."

Do not let busyness get in the way of seeing others. Slow down and acknowledge other people. I promise everyone will benefit from the love.

ACKNOWLEDGE
PEOPLE

COACH YOURSELF

We humans are sooooo good at giving advice to others yet when it comes to our own circumstances we are lost. So, the best way to answer our own questions is to actually encourage someone to coach themself.

More often than not the answer we seek is right there in our heart and available to us if we just stop and listen. Ask the person "What would you tell your best friend in this situation?" or "What do you think I should say to you?" or "What is it you'd like to hear me say?" These open up an invitation for someone to listen to their own wisdom.

Not only can you do this for others. You can do this for yourself too. When you are feeling stuck with something take a step back and say "What would my coach say to do here?" and see what insights you glean from this inquiry.

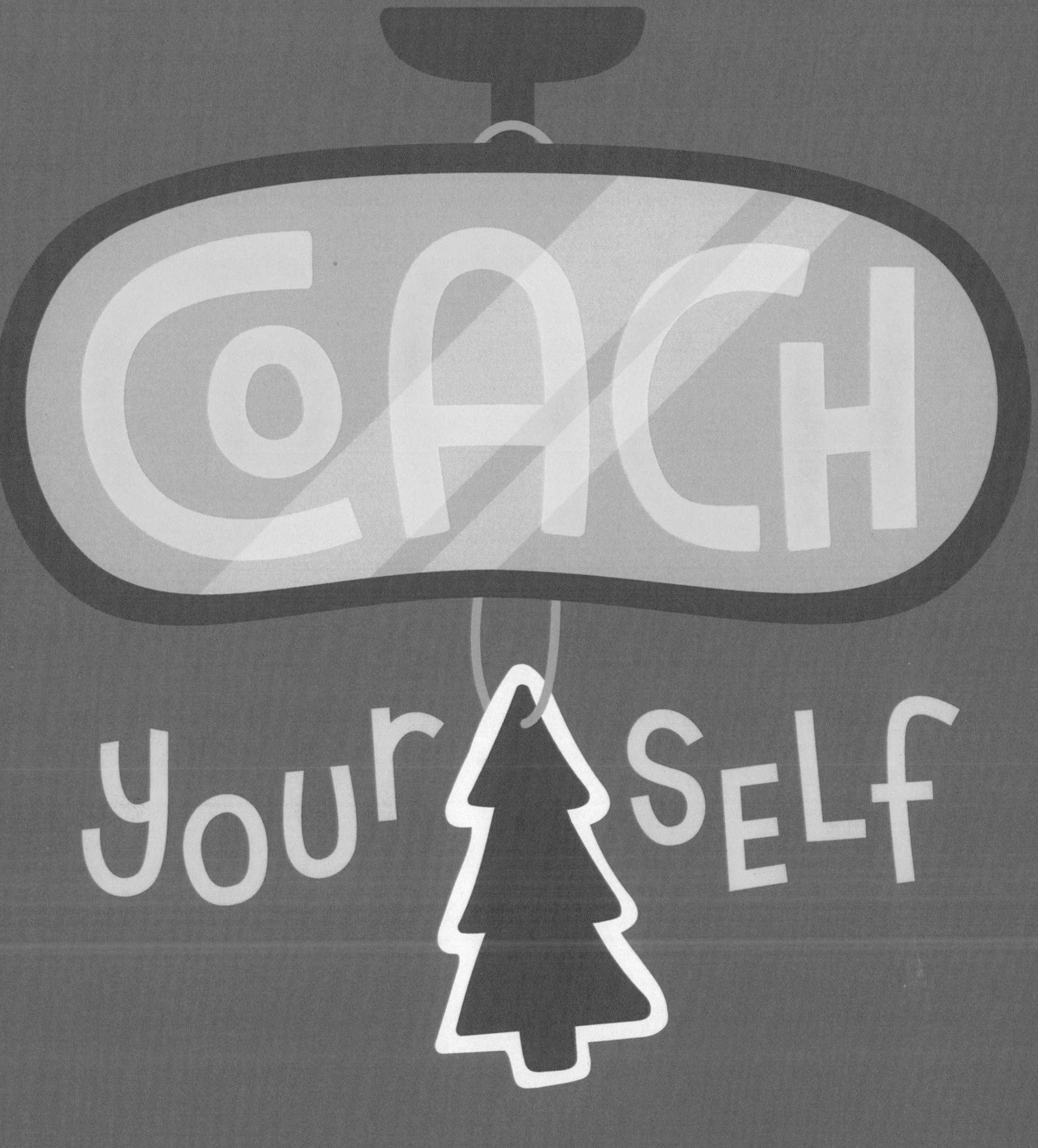
COACH
yourSELF

CELEBRATE YOUR SUCCESSES

In this busy world we jump from one goal to the next without stopping to celebrate. Why even go towards a goal if you don't even take time to enjoy it?

Also, set milestones to celebrate along the way. This will keep the energy directed towards your dreams and help move you towards success. Plus, it just feels good to celebrate even the smallest wins. One day those small accomplishments may be the biggest steps towards your success.

celebrate

YOUR

SUCCESSES

IT'S TIME TO KEEP SHUCKING!

The world needs your pearl to shine. When it does, it makes the whole world brighter!!! Plus, when you shine, it gives others permission to sparkle too!

Download the Art of Shucking guide to learn even more life changing tools and techniques based on love to live your best life at www.lifeshucker.com.

Sign up to receive the Pearls of Wisdom newsletter to support you in living a life you love at www.lifeshucker.com.

Join the shucking family @JessicaZemple on Instagram and Facebook to remind you just how shucktacular you are!

  @JessicaZemple

www.lifeshucker.com

CPSIA information can be obtained
at www.ICGtesting.com
Printed in the USA
LVRC092123140421
684581LV00001B/1

9 781734 682915